50 Irish Farmhouse Recipes for Home

By: Kelly Johnson

Table of Contents

- Irish Stew
- Boxty (Irish Potato Pancakes)
- Colcannon (Mashed Potatoes with Cabbage)
- Soda Bread
- Beef and Guinness Pie
- Dublin Coddle
- Shepherd's Pie
- Irish Potato Soup
- Barmbrack (Irish Fruit Bread)
- Bacon and Cabbage
- Potato Farls
- Champ (Mashed Potatoes with Spring Onions)
- Irish Apple Cake
- Guinness Beef Stew
- Irish Coffee
- Irish Soda Farls
- Carrageen Moss Pudding
- Salmon with Dill Sauce
- Black Pudding
- Irish Whiskey Cake
- Boxty Bread
- Dublin Lawyer (Lobster in Whiskey Cream Sauce)
- Dublin Bay Prawns with Garlic Butter
- Irish Oatcakes
- Irish Lamb Stew
- Potato Leek Soup
- Boxty Dumplings
- Irish Tea Brack
- Colcannon Soup
- Seafood Chowder
- Boxty Rolls
- Bacon and Potato Bake
- Irish Sausages with Onion Gravy
- Beef and Stout Stew
- Kerry Apple Cake

- Irish Brown Bread
- Smoked Salmon with Brown Bread
- Boxty Pancakes with Smoked Salmon
- Irish Coffee Cake
- Irish Leek and Potato Gratin
- Rhubarb Crumble
- Boxty Fritters
- Irish Cheese Platter
- Dubliner Cheese and Onion Tart
- Potato Bread
- Irish Lamb Shank with Mint Sauce
- Boxty with Fried Eggs
- Roast Chicken with Bacon and Potatoes
- Dublin Lawyer Pasta
- Chocolate Guinness Cake

Irish Stew

Ingredients:

- 2 lbs (about 900g) lamb shoulder, cut into chunks
- 4 large potatoes, peeled and cut into chunks
- 2 large carrots, peeled and sliced
- 2 onions, chopped
- 2 cloves garlic, minced
- 4 cups (about 1 liter) beef or lamb broth
- 2 tablespoons tomato paste
- 2 bay leaves
- 1 teaspoon dried thyme
- Salt and pepper to taste
- Chopped fresh parsley for garnish (optional)

Instructions:

1. In a large pot or Dutch oven, heat some oil over medium-high heat. Add the lamb chunks and brown them on all sides, about 5 minutes. Remove the lamb from the pot and set aside.
2. In the same pot, add a little more oil if needed, then add the chopped onions and garlic. Cook until the onions are softened and translucent, about 5 minutes.
3. Return the browned lamb to the pot. Add the potatoes, carrots, bay leaves, dried thyme, tomato paste, and beef or lamb broth. Season with salt and pepper to taste.
4. Bring the stew to a boil, then reduce the heat to low. Cover and simmer for about 1.5 to 2 hours, or until the lamb is tender and the vegetables are cooked through. Stir occasionally to prevent sticking.
5. Once the stew is cooked, taste and adjust seasoning if needed. Remove the bay leaves.
6. Serve the Irish Stew hot, garnished with chopped fresh parsley if desired. Enjoy with some crusty bread or Irish soda bread on the side.

This hearty and comforting Irish Stew is perfect for chilly evenings and will surely warm you up from the inside out!

Boxty (Irish Potato Pancakes)

Ingredients:

- 2 cups grated raw potatoes
- 2 cups mashed potatoes (leftover mashed potatoes work well)
- 1 cup all-purpose flour
- 1 teaspoon baking powder
- 1 teaspoon salt
- 1/2 cup milk
- 2 tablespoons butter, melted (plus extra for frying)
- Optional: chopped fresh herbs such as parsley or chives

Instructions:

1. Start by grating the raw potatoes using a box grater. Place the grated potatoes in a clean kitchen towel and squeeze out as much liquid as possible. Transfer the grated potatoes to a large mixing bowl.
2. Add the mashed potatoes to the grated potatoes in the mixing bowl.
3. In a separate bowl, sift together the all-purpose flour, baking powder, and salt.
4. Gradually add the dry ingredients to the potato mixture, stirring until well combined.
5. Stir in the milk and melted butter until a thick batter forms. If desired, add chopped fresh herbs for extra flavor.
6. Heat a skillet or frying pan over medium heat and add a small amount of butter to coat the bottom.
7. Drop spoonfuls of the Boxty batter onto the hot skillet, using the back of the spoon to spread the batter into circles. Cook for 2-3 minutes on each side, or until golden brown and crispy.
8. Remove the cooked Boxty pancakes from the skillet and place them on a plate lined with paper towels to absorb any excess grease.
9. Continue cooking the remaining batter in batches, adding more butter to the skillet as needed.
10. Serve the Boxty pancakes hot, with toppings such as sour cream, applesauce, or smoked salmon, if desired.

These crispy and flavorful Irish Potato Pancakes are perfect for breakfast, brunch, or as a side dish with your favorite savory meals. Enjoy!

Colcannon (Mashed Potatoes with Cabbage)

Ingredients:

- 2 lbs (about 900g) potatoes, peeled and diced
- 1 small head of cabbage, shredded
- 4 tablespoons butter (plus extra for serving)
- 1 cup milk or cream
- Salt and pepper to taste
- 4-5 scallions (green onions), finely chopped
- Optional: chopped parsley for garnish

Instructions:

1. Place the diced potatoes in a large pot and cover them with water. Add a pinch of salt to the water. Bring the water to a boil, then reduce the heat to medium-low and simmer the potatoes until they are fork-tender, about 15-20 minutes.
2. While the potatoes are cooking, place the shredded cabbage in another pot and cover it with water. Bring the water to a boil, then reduce the heat and simmer the cabbage until it is tender, about 5-7 minutes. Drain the cabbage well and set it aside.
3. Once the potatoes are cooked, drain them and return them to the pot. Mash the potatoes using a potato masher or a fork until they are smooth and free of lumps.
4. In a small saucepan, heat the milk or cream over medium heat until warm (do not boil). Add the warm milk to the mashed potatoes, along with the butter. Stir until the butter is melted and the potatoes are creamy. Season with salt and pepper to taste.
5. Add the cooked cabbage and chopped scallions to the mashed potatoes. Stir until the cabbage and scallions are evenly distributed throughout the mixture.
6. Transfer the Colcannon to a serving dish. Make a well in the center and add a knob of butter. Sprinkle with chopped parsley for garnish, if desired.
7. Serve the Colcannon hot as a side dish alongside your favorite meat or fish dishes.

This creamy and flavorful Colcannon is a perfect comfort food to enjoy on a cold day or as part of a traditional Irish meal. Enjoy!

Soda Bread

Ingredients:

- 4 cups all-purpose flour
- 1 teaspoon baking soda
- 1 teaspoon salt
- 1 3/4 cups buttermilk (or 1 3/4 cups milk mixed with 1 tablespoon white vinegar or lemon juice)

Optional add-ins:

- 1/2 to 1 cup raisins or currants
- 1 tablespoon caraway seeds
- 1 tablespoon sugar

Instructions:

1. Preheat your oven to 425°F (220°C). Lightly grease a baking sheet or line it with parchment paper.
2. In a large mixing bowl, whisk together the flour, baking soda, and salt. If you're adding any optional ingredients like raisins, currants, caraway seeds, or sugar, you can mix them in at this stage.
3. Make a well in the center of the dry ingredients and pour in the buttermilk. Using a wooden spoon or your hands, gently mix the ingredients until they come together to form a soft dough. Be careful not to overmix.
4. Turn the dough out onto a lightly floured surface and gently knead it for just a minute or two until it forms a round loaf. Shape it into a ball and place it onto the prepared baking sheet.
5. Using a sharp knife, score a deep cross into the top of the loaf. This helps the bread to bake evenly and allows steam to escape.
6. Bake the soda bread in the preheated oven for 15 minutes, then reduce the temperature to 400°F (200°C) and continue baking for an additional 25-30 minutes, or until the bread is golden brown and sounds hollow when tapped on the bottom.

7. Once baked, transfer the soda bread to a wire rack to cool completely before slicing and serving. Enjoy it fresh with butter, jam, or alongside soups and stews.

This Irish Soda Bread is best enjoyed the day it's made, but it can also be sliced and frozen for later enjoyment. It's perfect for breakfast, brunch, or as a tasty accompaniment to any meal!

Beef and Guinness Pie

Ingredients:

For the filling:

- 2 lbs (about 900g) beef chuck or stewing beef, cut into cubes
- 2 tablespoons all-purpose flour
- Salt and pepper to taste
- 2 tablespoons olive oil
- 1 onion, chopped
- 2 cloves garlic, minced
- 2 carrots, diced
- 2 celery stalks, diced
- 1 cup Guinness stout
- 1 cup beef broth
- 2 tablespoons tomato paste
- 1 tablespoon Worcestershire sauce
- 1 teaspoon dried thyme
- 1 bay leaf
- 1 tablespoon cornstarch (optional, for thickening)

For the pastry crust:

- 2 sheets of store-bought puff pastry, thawed
- 1 egg, beaten (for egg wash)

Instructions:

1. Preheat your oven to 375°F (190°C).
2. In a large bowl, toss the beef cubes with the flour, salt, and pepper until evenly coated.
3. Heat the olive oil in a large oven-safe pot or Dutch oven over medium-high heat. Add the beef cubes in batches and brown them on all sides. Remove the browned beef cubes from the pot and set them aside.

4. In the same pot, add the chopped onion, minced garlic, diced carrots, and diced celery. Cook, stirring occasionally, until the vegetables are softened, about 5 minutes.
5. Return the browned beef cubes to the pot. Pour in the Guinness stout, beef broth, tomato paste, Worcestershire sauce, dried thyme, and bay leaf. Stir to combine.
6. Bring the mixture to a simmer, then cover the pot and transfer it to the preheated oven. Let it cook in the oven for 1.5 to 2 hours, or until the beef is tender and the sauce has thickened. If the sauce needs further thickening, you can mix the cornstarch with a little water and stir it into the pot during the last 15 minutes of cooking.
7. While the filling is cooking, prepare the pastry crust. Roll out one sheet of puff pastry on a lightly floured surface to fit the size of your pie dish.
8. Once the filling is ready, remove the bay leaf and discard it. Pour the beef and Guinness mixture into a pie dish.
9. Place the rolled-out puff pastry sheet over the top of the pie dish, trimming any excess pastry. Brush the pastry with the beaten egg to create a golden finish.
10. Cut a few slits in the pastry to allow steam to escape during baking.
11. Bake the Beef and Guinness Pie in the preheated oven for 25-30 minutes, or until the pastry is puffed and golden brown.
12. Allow the pie to cool for a few minutes before serving. Slice and serve warm, with mashed potatoes and green peas, if desired.

This Beef and Guinness Pie is a comforting and satisfying dish, perfect for a cozy dinner on a chilly evening. Enjoy!

Dublin Coddle

Ingredients:

- 8 pork sausages (preferably Irish or your favorite sausage variety)
- 8 slices of bacon, chopped into bite-sized pieces
- 2 large onions, sliced
- 4 large potatoes, peeled and sliced into thick rounds
- 2 cups (about 500ml) chicken or vegetable broth
- 2 bay leaves
- Salt and pepper to taste
- Chopped fresh parsley for garnish (optional)

Instructions:

1. Preheat your oven to 350°F (175°C).
2. In a large skillet or frying pan, cook the bacon pieces over medium heat until they are browned and crispy. Remove the bacon from the pan and set it aside, leaving the bacon drippings in the pan.
3. Add the sausages to the same skillet and brown them on all sides. Once browned, remove the sausages from the pan and set them aside.
4. In a large oven-safe pot or Dutch oven, layer half of the sliced onions on the bottom of the pot.
5. Arrange half of the sliced potatoes on top of the onions, followed by half of the browned sausages and bacon pieces. Repeat the layers with the remaining onions, potatoes, sausages, and bacon.
6. Pour the chicken or vegetable broth over the layered ingredients in the pot. Add the bay leaves, and season with salt and pepper to taste.
7. Cover the pot with a lid and transfer it to the preheated oven. Let the Dublin Coddle bake in the oven for about 1.5 to 2 hours, or until the potatoes are tender and the flavors have melded together.
8. Once the Dublin Coddle is cooked, remove it from the oven and discard the bay leaves.
9. Serve the Dublin Coddle hot, garnished with chopped fresh parsley if desired. Enjoy with some crusty bread or Irish soda bread on the side.

This Dublin Coddle is a comforting and satisfying dish, perfect for a cozy dinner on a cold evening. It's a classic example of Irish farmhouse cooking at its best!

Shepherd's Pie

Ingredients:

For the mashed potato topping:

- 2 lbs (about 900g) potatoes, peeled and cut into chunks
- 4 tablespoons butter
- 1/2 cup milk or cream
- Salt and pepper to taste
- Optional: grated cheese for topping

For the filling:

- 1 tablespoon olive oil
- 1 onion, chopped
- 2 cloves garlic, minced
- 2 carrots, diced
- 2 celery stalks, diced
- 1 lb (about 450g) ground lamb or beef
- 2 tablespoons all-purpose flour
- 1 cup beef or vegetable broth
- 2 tablespoons tomato paste
- 1 teaspoon Worcestershire sauce
- 1 teaspoon dried thyme
- Salt and pepper to taste
- 1 cup frozen peas
- Chopped fresh parsley for garnish (optional)

Instructions:

1. Preheat your oven to 375°F (190°C).
2. Place the potatoes in a large pot and cover them with water. Bring the water to a boil, then reduce the heat to medium-low and simmer the potatoes until they are fork-tender, about 15-20 minutes.

3. While the potatoes are cooking, heat the olive oil in a large skillet over medium heat. Add the chopped onion, minced garlic, diced carrots, and diced celery. Cook, stirring occasionally, until the vegetables are softened, about 5-7 minutes.
4. Add the ground lamb or beef to the skillet. Cook, breaking up the meat with a spoon, until it is browned and cooked through.
5. Sprinkle the flour over the meat and vegetables in the skillet. Stir to combine and cook for another minute.
6. Pour in the beef or vegetable broth, tomato paste, Worcestershire sauce, and dried thyme. Stir well to combine and bring the mixture to a simmer. Cook for a few minutes until the sauce thickens slightly. Season with salt and pepper to taste.
7. Stir in the frozen peas and cook for another minute, then remove the skillet from the heat.
8. Once the potatoes are cooked, drain them and return them to the pot. Add the butter and milk or cream to the pot. Mash the potatoes until smooth and creamy. Season with salt and pepper to taste.
9. Transfer the meat and vegetable mixture to a large baking dish. Spread the mashed potatoes evenly over the top, using a spoon or spatula to create a smooth surface. If desired, sprinkle grated cheese over the top of the mashed potatoes.
10. Place the Shepherd's Pie in the preheated oven and bake for 25-30 minutes, or until the top is golden brown and the filling is bubbling.
11. Remove the Shepherd's Pie from the oven and let it cool for a few minutes before serving. Garnish with chopped fresh parsley, if desired.

This Shepherd's Pie is a comforting and satisfying dish that's perfect for a family dinner or gathering with friends. Enjoy!

Irish Potato Soup

Ingredients:

- 4 tablespoons butter
- 1 onion, chopped
- 2 cloves garlic, minced
- 4 cups (about 900g) potatoes, peeled and diced
- 4 cups (about 1 liter) chicken or vegetable broth
- 1 cup (about 240ml) milk or cream
- Salt and pepper to taste
- Optional toppings: chopped chives, grated cheese, crispy bacon bits

Instructions:

1. In a large pot, melt the butter over medium heat. Add the chopped onion and minced garlic to the pot. Cook, stirring occasionally, until the onion is softened and translucent, about 5 minutes.
2. Add the diced potatoes to the pot and stir to coat them in the buttery mixture.
3. Pour the chicken or vegetable broth into the pot, making sure the potatoes are submerged. Bring the mixture to a boil, then reduce the heat to medium-low and simmer for about 15-20 minutes, or until the potatoes are tender and easily pierced with a fork.
4. Once the potatoes are cooked, use an immersion blender to puree the soup until smooth and creamy. Alternatively, you can transfer the soup in batches to a blender and blend until smooth, then return it to the pot.
5. Stir in the milk or cream to the soup and heat it gently over low heat until warmed through. Be careful not to boil the soup once the dairy has been added.
6. Season the soup with salt and pepper to taste. Adjust the consistency by adding more broth or milk if desired.
7. Ladle the Irish Potato Soup into bowls and garnish with chopped chives, grated cheese, or crispy bacon bits if desired.
8. Serve the soup hot with crusty bread or Irish soda bread on the side.

This creamy and comforting Irish Potato Soup is sure to warm you up from the inside out. It's a perfect starter or a light meal on its own. Enjoy!

Barmbrack (Irish Fruit Bread)

Ingredients:

- 2 cups mixed dried fruits (such as raisins, currants, chopped dates, and chopped apricots)
- 1 cup hot black tea
- 1/4 cup whiskey or Irish whiskey (optional)
- 2 cups all-purpose flour
- 1 teaspoon baking powder
- 1/2 teaspoon baking soda
- 1/2 teaspoon ground cinnamon
- 1/4 teaspoon ground nutmeg
- 1/4 teaspoon ground cloves
- 1/4 teaspoon salt
- 1/2 cup brown sugar
- Zest of 1 orange
- Zest of 1 lemon
- 2 eggs, beaten
- 1/4 cup melted butter or vegetable oil

Instructions:

1. In a large bowl, combine the mixed dried fruits, hot black tea, and whiskey (if using). Let the mixture soak for at least 1 hour, or preferably overnight, until the fruits are plump and rehydrated.
2. Preheat your oven to 350°F (175°C). Grease and flour a loaf pan or line it with parchment paper.
3. In a separate bowl, sift together the all-purpose flour, baking powder, baking soda, ground cinnamon, ground nutmeg, ground cloves, and salt.
4. Stir in the brown sugar and citrus zest (orange and lemon) into the dry ingredients until well combined.
5. In another bowl, whisk together the beaten eggs and melted butter or vegetable oil.
6. Gradually add the wet ingredients to the dry ingredients, stirring until a thick batter forms. Fold in the soaked dried fruits along with any remaining liquid.
7. Pour the batter into the prepared loaf pan, spreading it evenly with a spatula.

8. Bake the Barmbrack in the preheated oven for 50-60 minutes, or until a toothpick inserted into the center comes out clean.
9. Remove the bread from the oven and let it cool in the pan for 10 minutes before transferring it to a wire rack to cool completely.
10. Once cooled, slice the Barmbrack and serve it with butter, if desired. Enjoy it with a cup of tea or coffee!

This Barmbrack is wonderfully moist and packed with fruity flavors, making it a delightful treat for breakfast or snack time.

Bacon and Cabbage

Ingredients:

- 1 head of cabbage
- 4-6 slices of bacon (Irish bacon or back bacon works well)
- 2-3 tablespoons butter
- Salt and pepper to taste

Instructions:

1. Start by preparing the cabbage. Remove any tough or discolored outer leaves from the cabbage, then slice it into wedges, cutting through the core. Rinse the cabbage wedges under cold water and set them aside to drain.
2. In a large pot, bring water to a boil. Add a pinch of salt to the water.
3. Carefully add the cabbage wedges to the boiling water. Cook them for about 5-7 minutes, or until they are tender but still slightly crisp. Be careful not to overcook the cabbage, as it can become mushy.
4. While the cabbage is cooking, cook the bacon slices in a separate skillet over medium heat until they are crispy. Once cooked, remove the bacon from the skillet and set it aside.
5. In the same skillet, melt the butter over medium heat. Add the cooked cabbage wedges to the skillet, tossing them in the butter to coat evenly. Season with salt and pepper to taste.
6. Cook the cabbage in the butter for a few minutes, allowing it to absorb the flavors.
7. Once the cabbage is heated through and well coated with butter, transfer it to a serving platter.
8. Crumble the cooked bacon slices over the top of the cabbage.
9. Serve the Bacon and Cabbage hot as a side dish alongside your favorite main course.

This Bacon and Cabbage dish is wonderfully savory and makes a perfect accompaniment to a variety of meals. Enjoy its comforting flavors!

Potato Farls

Ingredients:

- 2 cups mashed potatoes (about 2 medium-sized potatoes)
- 1 cup all-purpose flour, plus extra for dusting
- 1/2 teaspoon salt
- 2 tablespoons butter, melted (optional)
- Butter or oil for frying

Instructions:

1. Start by preparing the mashed potatoes. Peel the potatoes and cut them into chunks. Boil them in salted water until they are fork-tender. Drain the potatoes and mash them until smooth. Let them cool slightly.
2. In a large mixing bowl, combine the mashed potatoes, flour, and salt. Mix until a dough forms. If the dough is too sticky, add a little more flour until it becomes manageable.
3. Turn the dough out onto a floured surface. Knead it gently for a few minutes until it's smooth and elastic.
4. Divide the dough into four equal portions. Roll each portion into a ball, then flatten it into a disc about 1/4 inch thick.
5. Heat a skillet or griddle over medium heat and add a little butter or oil.
6. Carefully transfer the potato farls to the hot skillet. Cook them for about 3-4 minutes on each side, or until they are golden brown and cooked through. You may need to adjust the heat to prevent them from burning.
7. Once cooked, remove the potato farls from the skillet and transfer them to a plate lined with paper towels to absorb any excess oil.
8. Repeat the process with the remaining dough portions, adding more butter or oil to the skillet as needed.
9. Serve the potato farls hot, either on their own or as a side dish with breakfast or any meal. You can also brush them with melted butter for extra flavor if desired.

These Potato Farls are simple to make and have a wonderfully comforting texture. Enjoy them as a tasty addition to your Irish-inspired meals!

Champ (Mashed Potatoes with Spring Onions)

Ingredients:

- 2 lbs (about 900g) potatoes, peeled and quartered
- 1/2 cup milk
- 4 tablespoons butter, plus extra for serving
- 4-6 spring onions (scallions), finely chopped
- Salt and pepper to taste
- Optional: chopped fresh parsley for garnish

Instructions:

1. Place the peeled and quartered potatoes in a large pot and cover them with cold water. Add a pinch of salt to the water.
2. Bring the water to a boil, then reduce the heat to medium-low and simmer the potatoes until they are fork-tender, about 15-20 minutes.
3. While the potatoes are cooking, heat the milk and butter together in a small saucepan over low heat until the butter is melted and the mixture is warm. Set it aside.
4. Once the potatoes are cooked, drain them well and return them to the pot.
5. Mash the potatoes using a potato masher or a fork until they are smooth and free of lumps.
6. Gradually pour the warm milk and butter mixture into the mashed potatoes, stirring continuously until the potatoes are creamy and well combined. You may not need to use all of the milk and butter mixture, so add it gradually until you reach your desired consistency.
7. Stir in the finely chopped spring onions (scallions) until they are evenly distributed throughout the mashed potatoes.
8. Season the champ with salt and pepper to taste. Adjust the seasoning if necessary.
9. Transfer the champ to a serving bowl. Make a well in the center and add a knob of butter.
10. If desired, garnish the champ with chopped fresh parsley for a pop of color and flavor.
11. Serve the champ hot, with additional butter on top if desired.

This creamy and flavorful Champ is a perfect side dish to serve alongside roasted meats, stews, or any Irish-inspired meal. Enjoy its comforting and hearty flavors!

Irish Apple Cake

Ingredients:

For the cake:

- 2 cups all-purpose flour
- 1 teaspoon baking powder
- 1/2 teaspoon baking soda
- 1/2 teaspoon ground cinnamon
- 1/4 teaspoon ground nutmeg
- 1/4 teaspoon salt
- 1/2 cup (1 stick) unsalted butter, softened
- 3/4 cup granulated sugar
- 2 large eggs
- 1 teaspoon vanilla extract
- 1/2 cup buttermilk
- 2 cups peeled and diced apples (about 2 medium-sized apples)

For the topping:

- 2 tablespoons granulated sugar
- 1/2 teaspoon ground cinnamon

Instructions:

1. Preheat your oven to 350°F (175°C). Grease and flour a 9-inch round cake pan or springform pan.
2. In a medium bowl, sift together the flour, baking powder, baking soda, cinnamon, nutmeg, and salt. Set aside.
3. In a large mixing bowl, cream together the softened butter and granulated sugar until light and fluffy.
4. Beat in the eggs, one at a time, until well combined. Stir in the vanilla extract.

5. Gradually add the dry ingredients to the wet ingredients, alternating with the buttermilk, beginning and ending with the dry ingredients. Mix until just combined, being careful not to overmix.
6. Gently fold in the diced apples until evenly distributed throughout the batter.
7. Pour the batter into the prepared cake pan, spreading it evenly with a spatula.
8. In a small bowl, mix together the granulated sugar and ground cinnamon for the topping. Sprinkle the mixture evenly over the top of the cake batter.
9. Bake the Irish Apple Cake in the preheated oven for 35-40 minutes, or until a toothpick inserted into the center comes out clean and the top is golden brown.
10. Remove the cake from the oven and let it cool in the pan for 10 minutes. Then, carefully transfer it to a wire rack to cool completely.
11. Once cooled, slice the Irish Apple Cake and serve it on its own or with a dollop of whipped cream or a scoop of vanilla ice cream.

This Irish Apple Cake is moist, tender, and bursting with the flavors of cinnamon-spiced apples. It's a perfect dessert for any occasion, whether you're celebrating St. Patrick's Day or simply craving a taste of Ireland. Enjoy!

Guinness Beef Stew

Ingredients:

- 2 lbs (about 900g) beef chuck or stewing beef, cut into 1-inch cubes
- Salt and pepper to taste
- 2 tablespoons olive oil
- 2 onions, chopped
- 4 cloves garlic, minced
- 4 carrots, peeled and sliced
- 4 celery stalks, sliced
- 2 tablespoons tomato paste
- 2 cups beef broth
- 1 (14.9 oz) can Guinness stout
- 2 bay leaves
- 1 teaspoon dried thyme
- 1 teaspoon dried rosemary
- 2 tablespoons all-purpose flour (optional, for thickening)
- Chopped fresh parsley for garnish (optional)

Instructions:

1. Season the beef cubes with salt and pepper to taste.
2. Heat the olive oil in a large pot or Dutch oven over medium-high heat. Add the beef cubes in batches and brown them on all sides. Remove the browned beef from the pot and set it aside.
3. In the same pot, add the chopped onions and minced garlic. Cook until the onions are softened and translucent, about 5 minutes.
4. Add the sliced carrots and celery to the pot. Cook for another 5 minutes, stirring occasionally.
5. Return the browned beef to the pot. Stir in the tomato paste until well combined.
6. Pour in the beef broth and Guinness stout, scraping the bottom of the pot to release any browned bits.
7. Add the bay leaves, dried thyme, and dried rosemary to the pot. Stir to combine.
8. Bring the stew to a boil, then reduce the heat to low. Cover and simmer for about 2 hours, or until the beef is tender and the flavors have melded together.

9. If you prefer a thicker stew, you can mix the flour with a little water to create a slurry, then stir it into the stew during the last 15 minutes of cooking to thicken the sauce.
10. Once the stew is cooked, taste and adjust the seasoning if necessary. Remove the bay leaves.
11. Serve the Guinness Beef Stew hot, garnished with chopped fresh parsley if desired. Enjoy with crusty bread or mashed potatoes on the side.

This Guinness Beef Stew is rich, savory, and deeply satisfying, with the addition of Guinness stout adding a delicious depth of flavor. It's a perfect comfort food to enjoy during the cooler months!

Irish Coffee

Ingredients:

- 1 cup hot brewed coffee
- 1 1/2 oz (45ml) Irish whiskey
- 1 tablespoon brown sugar (or to taste)
- Whipped cream, for topping
- Ground cinnamon or nutmeg, for garnish (optional)

Instructions:

1. Start by brewing a cup of strong coffee using your preferred method.
2. While the coffee is brewing, preheat a heatproof glass or mug by filling it with hot water. Let it sit for a minute, then discard the water.
3. Pour the hot brewed coffee into the preheated glass or mug, filling it about three-quarters full.
4. Add the Irish whiskey and brown sugar to the coffee. Stir well until the sugar is dissolved.
5. Gently float a layer of whipped cream on top of the coffee. You can either spoon the whipped cream over the back of a spoon to create a layer, or use a cream whipper for a denser foam.
6. Optionally, sprinkle a pinch of ground cinnamon or nutmeg over the whipped cream for garnish.
7. Serve the Irish Coffee immediately, with a spoon for stirring if desired.

Irish Coffee is a delightful combination of warm coffee, smooth whiskey, and creamy whipped cream, making it the perfect after-dinner drink or cozy treat on a chilly evening. Enjoy responsibly!

Irish Soda Farls

Ingredients:

- 1 cup hot brewed coffee
- 1 1/2 oz (45ml) Irish whiskey
- 1 tablespoon brown sugar (or to taste)
- Whipped cream, for topping
- Ground cinnamon or nutmeg, for garnish (optional)

Instructions:

1. Start by brewing a cup of strong coffee using your preferred method.
2. While the coffee is brewing, preheat a heatproof glass or mug by filling it with hot water. Let it sit for a minute, then discard the water.
3. Pour the hot brewed coffee into the preheated glass or mug, filling it about three-quarters full.
4. Add the Irish whiskey and brown sugar to the coffee. Stir well until the sugar is dissolved.
5. Gently float a layer of whipped cream on top of the coffee. You can either spoon the whipped cream over the back of a spoon to create a layer, or use a cream whipper for a denser foam.
6. Optionally, sprinkle a pinch of ground cinnamon or nutmeg over the whipped cream for garnish.
7. Serve the Irish Coffee immediately, with a spoon for stirring if desired.

Irish Coffee is a delightful combination of warm coffee, smooth whiskey, and creamy whipped cream, making it the perfect after-dinner drink or cozy treat on a chilly evening. Enjoy responsibly!

Carrageen Moss Pudding

Ingredients:

- 1/4 cup dried carrageen moss (Irish moss)
- 2 cups whole milk
- 2 cups heavy cream
- 1/4 cup sugar
- 1 teaspoon vanilla extract
- Optional toppings: honey, fruit compote, whipped cream, or fresh berries

Instructions:

1. Start by rinsing the dried carrageen moss under cold water to remove any debris or salt.
2. In a medium saucepan, combine the rinsed carrageen moss, whole milk, and heavy cream. Bring the mixture to a gentle simmer over medium heat, stirring occasionally.
3. Once the mixture reaches a simmer, reduce the heat to low and let it simmer gently for about 15-20 minutes, stirring occasionally. The carrageen moss will soften and release its natural gelatin, thickening the mixture.
4. After simmering, remove the saucepan from the heat and strain the mixture through a fine-mesh sieve or cheesecloth to remove the carrageen moss solids. Press down gently to extract as much liquid as possible.
5. Return the strained mixture to the saucepan and place it back over low heat. Stir in the sugar and vanilla extract until the sugar is dissolved. Taste and adjust the sweetness if necessary.
6. Continue to cook the pudding mixture over low heat for another 5-10 minutes, stirring constantly, until it thickens to a custard-like consistency.
7. Once thickened, remove the pudding from the heat and pour it into individual serving dishes or a large serving bowl.
8. Let the pudding cool to room temperature, then cover and refrigerate it for at least 2-3 hours, or until chilled and set.
9. Serve the Carrageen Moss Pudding cold, with optional toppings such as a drizzle of honey, fruit compote, whipped cream, or fresh berries.

Carrageen Moss Pudding is a unique and traditional Irish dessert with a delicate texture and subtle flavor. Enjoy its creamy goodness as a refreshing treat after a hearty meal!

Salmon with Dill Sauce

Ingredients:

For the salmon:

- 4 salmon fillets (about 6 ounces each), skin-on or skinless
- Salt and pepper to taste
- 1 tablespoon olive oil

For the dill sauce:

- 1/2 cup mayonnaise
- 1/4 cup sour cream or Greek yogurt
- 2 tablespoons chopped fresh dill
- 1 tablespoon lemon juice
- 1 teaspoon Dijon mustard
- Salt and pepper to taste

Instructions:

1. Preheat your oven to 400°F (200°C). Line a baking sheet with parchment paper or aluminum foil for easy cleanup.
2. Pat the salmon fillets dry with paper towels and season them with salt and pepper on both sides.
3. Heat the olive oil in a large oven-safe skillet over medium-high heat. Once the skillet is hot, add the salmon fillets to the skillet, skin-side down if using skin-on fillets. Sear the salmon for 2-3 minutes until golden brown on the bottom.
4. Carefully transfer the skillet to the preheated oven. Bake the salmon for 8-10 minutes, or until it flakes easily with a fork and reaches your desired level of doneness.
5. While the salmon is baking, prepare the dill sauce. In a small bowl, whisk together the mayonnaise, sour cream or Greek yogurt, chopped fresh dill, lemon juice, and Dijon mustard until smooth and well combined. Season with salt and pepper to taste.
6. Once the salmon is cooked, remove it from the oven and let it rest for a few minutes.

7. Serve the salmon fillets hot, topped with a generous spoonful of dill sauce. Garnish with additional fresh dill, if desired.
8. Enjoy your delicious Salmon with Dill Sauce with your favorite side dishes, such as roasted potatoes, steamed vegetables, or a crisp green salad.

This Salmon with Dill Sauce is a simple yet elegant dish that's perfect for any occasion, from weeknight dinners to special gatherings. The creamy dill sauce adds a burst of flavor that complements the tender and flaky salmon beautifully.

Black Pudding

Ingredients:

- 1 lb (about 450g) fresh pork blood (available from specialty butchers)
- 1 cup steel-cut oats or barley
- 1 large onion, finely chopped
- 1/2 teaspoon ground cloves
- 1/2 teaspoon ground allspice
- 1/2 teaspoon ground nutmeg
- Salt and pepper to taste
- Pork fat or bacon fat, for frying

Instructions:

1. In a large mixing bowl, combine the fresh pork blood, steel-cut oats or barley, finely chopped onion, ground cloves, ground allspice, ground nutmeg, salt, and pepper. Mix well until all the ingredients are thoroughly combined.
2. Let the mixture sit at room temperature for about 30 minutes to allow the oats or barley to absorb some of the liquid.
3. Meanwhile, prepare a large pot of water and bring it to a gentle simmer.
4. Once the mixture has rested, spoon it into sausage casings, tying off the ends to form individual sausages. If you don't have sausage casings, you can shape the mixture into patties or cook it loose in a frying pan.
5. Carefully lower the sausages into the simmering water, making sure they are fully submerged. Let them simmer gently for about 30-40 minutes, turning occasionally, until they are cooked through.
6. Remove the sausages from the water and let them cool slightly.
7. Once cooled, heat a frying pan over medium heat and add a little pork fat or bacon fat. Fry the sausages in the hot fat until they are crispy and browned on the outside, about 5 minutes per side.
8. Once cooked, remove the sausages from the pan and let them drain on paper towels.
9. Serve the black pudding hot, sliced into rounds or wedges, as part of a traditional breakfast or as a tasty addition to other meals.

This homemade black pudding has a rich and savory flavor, with warm spices adding depth to the dish. Enjoy it as a hearty and satisfying treat!

Irish Whiskey Cake

Ingredients:

- 1 cup (225g) unsalted butter, softened
- 1 cup (200g) granulated sugar
- 4 large eggs
- 2 cups (250g) all-purpose flour
- 1 teaspoon baking powder
- 1/4 teaspoon salt
- 1/4 cup (60ml) Irish whiskey (such as Jameson)
- 1/4 cup (60ml) milk
- Zest of 1 lemon
- Zest of 1 orange
- 1/2 cup (50g) chopped walnuts or pecans (optional)
- Confectioners' sugar for dusting (optional)

Instructions:

1. Preheat your oven to 350°F (175°C). Grease and flour a 9-inch round cake pan or bundt pan.
2. In a large mixing bowl, cream together the softened butter and granulated sugar until light and fluffy.
3. Beat in the eggs, one at a time, until well combined.
4. In a separate bowl, sift together the all-purpose flour, baking powder, and salt.
5. Gradually add the dry ingredients to the butter mixture, alternating with the Irish whiskey and milk. Mix until just combined.
6. Stir in the lemon zest, orange zest, and chopped nuts (if using) until evenly distributed throughout the batter.
7. Pour the batter into the prepared cake pan, spreading it evenly with a spatula.
8. Bake the Irish Whiskey Cake in the preheated oven for 35-40 minutes, or until a toothpick inserted into the center comes out clean and the top is golden brown.
9. Remove the cake from the oven and let it cool in the pan for 10 minutes. Then, carefully transfer it to a wire rack to cool completely.
10. Once cooled, dust the top of the cake with confectioners' sugar for a decorative finish, if desired.

11. Slice the Irish Whiskey Cake and serve it on its own or with a dollop of whipped cream or a scoop of vanilla ice cream.

This Irish Whiskey Cake is moist, tender, and bursting with flavor, making it the perfect dessert for St. Patrick's Day celebrations or any special occasion. Enjoy its rich and indulgent taste!

Boxty Bread

Ingredients:

- 2 cups mashed potatoes (about 2 medium-sized potatoes)
- 1 cup grated raw potatoes (about 1 medium-sized potato)
- 1 1/2 cups all-purpose flour
- 1 teaspoon baking soda
- Salt to taste
- 1/4 cup buttermilk or milk
- Butter or oil for frying

Instructions:

1. Start by preparing the mashed potatoes. Peel the potatoes and cut them into chunks. Boil them in salted water until they are fork-tender. Drain the potatoes and mash them until smooth. Let them cool slightly.
2. In a clean kitchen towel or cheesecloth, squeeze out any excess moisture from the grated raw potatoes.
3. In a large mixing bowl, combine the mashed potatoes, grated raw potatoes, all-purpose flour, baking soda, and salt. Mix until well combined.
4. Gradually add the buttermilk or milk to the mixture, stirring until a thick batter forms. You may need to adjust the amount of liquid depending on the consistency of the batter.
5. Heat a skillet or griddle over medium heat and add a little butter or oil to grease the surface.
6. Drop spoonfuls of the boxty batter onto the hot skillet, using the back of the spoon to spread them into rounds, about 1/4 inch thick.
7. Cook the boxty bread for 3-4 minutes on each side, or until golden brown and cooked through. You may need to adjust the heat to prevent burning.
8. Once cooked, transfer the boxty bread to a plate lined with paper towels to drain any excess oil.
9. Repeat the process with the remaining batter, adding more butter or oil to the skillet as needed.
10. Serve the boxty bread hot, with butter, jam, or your favorite toppings.

Boxty bread is delicious served as a side dish with breakfast, lunch, or dinner. Its hearty texture and rich potato flavor make it a comforting and satisfying addition to any meal. Enjoy!

Dublin Lawyer (Lobster in Whiskey Cream Sauce)

Ingredients:

- 2 lobster tails, thawed if frozen
- 2 tablespoons unsalted butter
- 2 cloves garlic, minced
- 1/4 cup Irish whiskey (such as Jameson)
- 1 cup heavy cream
- Salt and pepper to taste
- Chopped fresh parsley for garnish (optional)
- Lemon wedges for serving

Instructions:

1. Preheat your oven to 400°F (200°C).
2. Using kitchen shears, carefully cut through the top shell of each lobster tail, stopping at the base of the tail. Gently pull apart the shells, exposing the meat, and remove the vein running along the back.
3. Place the lobster tails on a baking sheet or in an oven-safe dish.
4. Melt 1 tablespoon of butter in a small saucepan over medium heat. Add the minced garlic and cook for 1-2 minutes until fragrant.
5. Pour in the Irish whiskey and let it simmer for another minute to cook off the alcohol.
6. Stir in the heavy cream and season with salt and pepper to taste. Let the sauce simmer for 5-7 minutes, or until slightly thickened.
7. Pour the whiskey cream sauce over the lobster tails, ensuring they are evenly coated.
8. Cut the remaining tablespoon of butter into small pieces and dot them over the lobster tails.
9. Bake the lobster tails in the preheated oven for 12-15 minutes, or until the lobster meat is opaque and cooked through.
10. Once cooked, remove the lobster tails from the oven and transfer them to serving plates.
11. Spoon some of the whiskey cream sauce over the lobster tails and garnish with chopped fresh parsley, if desired.

12. Serve the Dublin Lawyer hot with lemon wedges on the side for squeezing over the lobster meat.

This rich and indulgent dish is perfect for special occasions or as a decadent treat for seafood lovers. Enjoy the luxurious flavors of Dublin Lawyer!

Dublin Bay Prawns with Garlic Butter

Ingredients:

- 1 lb (450g) Dublin Bay prawns or large shrimp, peeled and deveined
- 4 tablespoons unsalted butter
- 4 cloves garlic, minced
- 2 tablespoons chopped fresh parsley
- 1 tablespoon lemon juice
- Salt and pepper to taste
- Lemon wedges for serving
- Crusty bread or rice for serving (optional)

Instructions:

1. Rinse the prawns under cold water and pat them dry with paper towels. Set aside.
2. In a large skillet or frying pan, melt the butter over medium heat.
3. Add the minced garlic to the melted butter and cook for 1-2 minutes until fragrant, but be careful not to let it brown.
4. Add the prawns to the skillet in a single layer. Cook them for 2-3 minutes on each side, or until they turn pink and opaque.
5. Stir in the chopped parsley and lemon juice, and season with salt and pepper to taste. Toss the prawns in the garlic butter sauce until they are evenly coated.
6. Once the prawns are cooked through and coated in the garlic butter sauce, remove the skillet from the heat.
7. Serve the Dublin Bay Prawns hot, garnished with additional chopped parsley and lemon wedges on the side.
8. Optionally, serve the prawns with crusty bread or over a bed of rice to soak up the delicious garlic butter sauce.

This Dublin Bay Prawns with Garlic Butter recipe is quick and easy to make, yet it's bursting with flavor. It's perfect for a special dinner or as a delightful appetizer for seafood lovers. Enjoy!

Irish Oatcakes

Ingredients:

- 2 cups (200g) rolled oats (not instant oats)
- 1/2 cup (60g) all-purpose flour
- 1/2 teaspoon baking soda
- 1/2 teaspoon salt
- 2 tablespoons unsalted butter, melted
- 1/4 cup (60ml) boiling water
- Additional flour for dusting

Instructions:

1. Preheat your oven to 350°F (175°C). Line a baking sheet with parchment paper or lightly grease it.
2. In a large mixing bowl, combine the rolled oats, all-purpose flour, baking soda, and salt. Mix well to combine.
3. Add the melted butter to the dry ingredients and mix until the mixture resembles coarse crumbs.
4. Gradually add the boiling water to the mixture, stirring constantly, until a dough forms. You may not need to use all of the water.
5. Turn the dough out onto a lightly floured surface and knead it gently until smooth.
6. Roll out the dough to a thickness of about 1/4 inch (6mm).
7. Use a cookie cutter or a knife to cut the dough into rounds or squares, or use a pastry wheel to cut it into wedges.
8. Transfer the oatcakes to the prepared baking sheet, leaving a little space between each one.
9. Bake the oatcakes in the preheated oven for 15-20 minutes, or until golden brown and crisp.
10. Remove the oatcakes from the oven and let them cool on the baking sheet for a few minutes before transferring them to a wire rack to cool completely.
11. Once cooled, store the oatcakes in an airtight container at room temperature for up to 1 week.

These Irish oatcakes are delicious served plain or topped with cheese, jam, or honey. They make a delightful snack or accompaniment to your favorite cheeses and spreads. Enjoy!

Irish Lamb Stew

Ingredients:

- 2 lbs (about 900g) lamb shoulder, trimmed and cut into chunks
- Salt and pepper to taste
- 2 tablespoons vegetable oil
- 2 onions, chopped
- 4 cloves garlic, minced
- 4 carrots, peeled and sliced
- 4 celery stalks, sliced
- 1 lb (about 450g) potatoes, peeled and diced
- 4 cups beef or lamb broth
- 2 bay leaves
- 1 teaspoon dried thyme
- 1 teaspoon dried rosemary
- Chopped fresh parsley for garnish (optional)

Instructions:

1. Season the lamb chunks with salt and pepper to taste.
2. Heat the vegetable oil in a large Dutch oven or heavy-bottomed pot over medium-high heat. Once the oil is hot, add the lamb chunks in batches and brown them on all sides. Remove the browned lamb from the pot and set it aside.
3. In the same pot, add the chopped onions and minced garlic. Cook for 3-4 minutes, stirring occasionally, until the onions are softened and translucent.
4. Add the sliced carrots, sliced celery, and diced potatoes to the pot. Cook for another 5 minutes, stirring occasionally.
5. Return the browned lamb to the pot. Pour in the beef or lamb broth, ensuring that the ingredients are submerged. Add the bay leaves, dried thyme, and dried rosemary.
6. Bring the stew to a boil, then reduce the heat to low. Cover the pot and let the stew simmer gently for about 1 1/2 to 2 hours, or until the lamb is tender and the vegetables are cooked through.
7. Taste the stew and adjust the seasoning with salt and pepper if necessary. Remove the bay leaves before serving.
8. Serve the Irish Lamb Stew hot, garnished with chopped fresh parsley if desired.

This Irish Lamb Stew is a delicious and comforting dish, perfect for a cozy dinner at home or for celebrating St. Patrick's Day. Enjoy its rich flavors and tender chunks of lamb!

Potato Leek Soup

Ingredients:

- 2 tablespoons unsalted butter
- 2 leeks, white and light green parts only, thinly sliced
- 3 cloves garlic, minced
- 3 large potatoes, peeled and diced
- 4 cups chicken or vegetable broth
- 1 bay leaf
- 1 teaspoon dried thyme
- Salt and pepper to taste
- 1/2 cup heavy cream or half-and-half
- Chopped fresh chives or parsley for garnish (optional)

Instructions:

1. In a large pot or Dutch oven, melt the butter over medium heat. Add the sliced leeks and minced garlic. Cook, stirring occasionally, until the leeks are soft and translucent, about 5 minutes.
2. Add the diced potatoes to the pot and cook for another 2-3 minutes, stirring occasionally.
3. Pour in the chicken or vegetable broth, making sure the potatoes are submerged. Add the bay leaf and dried thyme to the pot.
4. Bring the soup to a boil, then reduce the heat to low. Cover the pot and let the soup simmer gently for about 15-20 minutes, or until the potatoes are tender.
5. Once the potatoes are cooked through, remove the bay leaf from the pot. Use an immersion blender to puree the soup until smooth and creamy. Alternatively, you can transfer the soup in batches to a blender and blend until smooth, then return it to the pot.
6. Stir in the heavy cream or half-and-half until well combined. Season the soup with salt and pepper to taste.
7. Continue to simmer the soup for another 5-10 minutes to allow the flavors to meld together.
8. Serve the Potato Leek Soup hot, garnished with chopped fresh chives or parsley if desired.

This Potato Leek Soup is rich, creamy, and full of flavor, making it a comforting and satisfying dish for lunch or dinner. Enjoy it with a crusty bread roll or a side salad for a complete meal!

Boxty Dumplings

Ingredients:

- 2 cups grated raw potatoes
- 1 cup mashed potatoes
- 1 cup all-purpose flour
- 1 teaspoon baking powder
- Salt to taste
- 2-3 tablespoons unsalted butter or oil, for frying

Instructions:

1. Start by preparing the grated raw potatoes. Peel the potatoes and grate them using a box grater or a food processor. Place the grated potatoes in a clean kitchen towel or cheesecloth and squeeze out any excess moisture.
2. In a large mixing bowl, combine the grated raw potatoes, mashed potatoes, all-purpose flour, baking powder, and salt. Mix well until a dough forms. If the dough is too wet, you can add a little more flour.
3. Divide the dough into small portions and shape them into dumplings, about the size of golf balls.
4. Heat the unsalted butter or oil in a large skillet or frying pan over medium heat.
5. Once the butter is melted or the oil is hot, add the dumplings to the skillet, making sure not to overcrowd them. Flatten them slightly with a spatula.
6. Cook the dumplings for 4-5 minutes on each side, or until golden brown and crispy.
7. Once cooked, remove the dumplings from the skillet and drain them on paper towels to remove any excess oil.
8. Serve the Boxty Dumplings hot as a side dish or as part of a main meal, alongside your favorite meats and vegetables.

These Boxty Dumplings are crispy on the outside and tender on the inside, with a delicious potato flavor. They're a delightful addition to any Irish-inspired meal or a cozy comfort food dish. Enjoy!

Irish Tea Brack

Ingredients:

- 1 1/2 cups (350ml) hot black tea
- 1 cup (200g) mixed dried fruits (such as raisins, currants, sultanas, and chopped apricots)
- 1/2 cup (100g) brown sugar
- 2 cups (250g) all-purpose flour
- 1 teaspoon baking powder
- 1 teaspoon ground cinnamon
- 1/2 teaspoon ground nutmeg
- 1/4 teaspoon ground cloves
- Zest of 1 lemon
- Zest of 1 orange
- 1 large egg, beaten
- Butter or oil, for greasing

Instructions:

1. In a large mixing bowl, combine the hot black tea and mixed dried fruits. Stir well to combine, then cover the bowl and let the fruits soak for at least 1 hour, or overnight if possible.
2. Preheat your oven to 350°F (175°C). Grease and line a 9x5-inch (23x13cm) loaf pan with parchment paper.
3. In a separate bowl, sift together the all-purpose flour, baking powder, ground cinnamon, ground nutmeg, and ground cloves.
4. Stir the brown sugar, lemon zest, and orange zest into the soaked dried fruit mixture until well combined.
5. Gradually add the dry ingredients to the fruit mixture, stirring until just combined. Be careful not to overmix.
6. Stir in the beaten egg until evenly distributed throughout the batter.
7. Pour the batter into the prepared loaf pan, spreading it evenly with a spatula.
8. Bake the Irish Tea Brack in the preheated oven for 50-60 minutes, or until a toothpick inserted into the center comes out clean and the top is golden brown.
9. Remove the loaf from the oven and let it cool in the pan for 10 minutes. Then, carefully transfer it to a wire rack to cool completely.

10. Once cooled, slice the Irish Tea Brack and serve it on its own or with a spread of butter.

This Irish Tea Brack is moist, flavorful, and filled with the natural sweetness of the soaked dried fruits. Enjoy a slice with a cup of tea for a delightful treat!

Colcannon Soup

Ingredients:

- 4 slices bacon, chopped (optional)
- 2 tablespoons unsalted butter
- 1 onion, chopped
- 2 cloves garlic, minced
- 4 cups chicken or vegetable broth
- 4 cups potatoes, peeled and diced
- 4 cups cabbage, shredded
- 1 cup milk or cream
- Salt and pepper to taste
- Chopped fresh chives or parsley for garnish (optional)

Instructions:

1. If using bacon, cook the chopped bacon in a large soup pot or Dutch oven over medium heat until crisp. Remove the bacon with a slotted spoon and set it aside, leaving the bacon fat in the pot.
2. In the same pot, melt the butter over medium heat. Add the chopped onion and minced garlic. Cook for 3-4 minutes, or until the onions are softened and translucent.
3. Pour in the chicken or vegetable broth, scraping up any browned bits from the bottom of the pot. Add the diced potatoes to the pot and bring the mixture to a boil.
4. Reduce the heat to low and let the soup simmer gently for about 15 minutes, or until the potatoes are tender.
5. Add the shredded cabbage to the pot and simmer for another 5-10 minutes, or until the cabbage is wilted and tender.
6. Use an immersion blender to blend the soup until smooth, or transfer it in batches to a blender and blend until smooth.
7. Stir in the milk or cream until well combined. Season the soup with salt and pepper to taste.
8. If using, stir in the cooked bacon pieces.
9. Serve the Colcannon Soup hot, garnished with chopped fresh chives or parsley if desired.

This Colcannon Soup is creamy, flavorful, and filled with the comforting flavors of potatoes, cabbage, and onions. It's perfect for warming up on chilly days or celebrating Irish cuisine!

Seafood Chowder

Ingredients:

- 4 slices bacon, chopped (optional)
- 2 tablespoons unsalted butter
- 1 onion, diced
- 2 stalks celery, diced
- 2 carrots, diced
- 2 cloves garlic, minced
- 1/4 cup all-purpose flour
- 4 cups seafood or fish stock
- 2 cups milk or half-and-half
- 2 cups potatoes, peeled and diced
- 1 bay leaf
- 1 teaspoon dried thyme
- Salt and pepper to taste
- 1 lb mixed seafood (such as shrimp, scallops, fish fillets, and/or crab meat), chopped into bite-sized pieces
- 1/2 cup frozen corn kernels
- 1/2 cup frozen peas
- Chopped fresh parsley for garnish (optional)

Instructions:

1. If using bacon, cook the chopped bacon in a large soup pot or Dutch oven over medium heat until crisp. Remove the bacon with a slotted spoon and set it aside, leaving the bacon fat in the pot.
2. In the same pot, melt the butter over medium heat. Add the diced onion, celery, and carrots. Cook for 5-6 minutes, or until the vegetables are softened.
3. Add the minced garlic to the pot and cook for an additional 1-2 minutes, or until fragrant.
4. Sprinkle the flour over the vegetables and stir to combine. Cook for 1-2 minutes to cook off the raw flour taste.
5. Gradually pour in the seafood or fish stock, stirring constantly to prevent lumps from forming. Add the milk or half-and-half, diced potatoes, bay leaf, dried thyme, salt, and pepper to taste.

6. Bring the mixture to a simmer and let it cook for about 10-15 minutes, or until the potatoes are tender and cooked through.
7. Add the chopped seafood, frozen corn kernels, and frozen peas to the pot. Simmer for another 5-7 minutes, or until the seafood is cooked through and opaque.
8. Remove the bay leaf from the pot and discard.
9. Taste the chowder and adjust the seasoning with salt and pepper if necessary.
10. Ladle the Seafood Chowder into bowls and garnish with chopped fresh parsley and reserved cooked bacon (if using) before serving.

This Seafood Chowder is creamy, flavorful, and filled with a variety of seafood and vegetables. It's perfect for a comforting and satisfying meal, especially on cold days or during seafood cravings!

Boxty Rolls

Ingredients:

- 2 cups grated raw potatoes
- 1 cup mashed potatoes
- 1 cup all-purpose flour
- 1 teaspoon baking powder
- Salt to taste
- 2-3 tablespoons unsalted butter, melted
- Butter or oil for greasing
- Fillings of your choice (e.g., cooked bacon, sautéed mushrooms, sliced cheese, cooked sausage, etc.)

Instructions:

1. Start by preparing the grated raw potatoes. Peel the potatoes and grate them using a box grater or a food processor. Place the grated potatoes in a clean kitchen towel or cheesecloth and squeeze out any excess moisture.
2. In a large mixing bowl, combine the grated raw potatoes, mashed potatoes, all-purpose flour, baking powder, and salt. Mix well until a dough forms. If the dough is too wet, you can add a little more flour.
3. Preheat your oven to 400°F (200°C). Grease a baking sheet with butter or oil.
4. Divide the dough into equal portions and shape each portion into a ball. Flatten each ball slightly into a disc shape.
5. Place your desired fillings in the center of each dough disc. Be careful not to overfill.
6. Fold the edges of the dough over the fillings, pinching them together to seal.
7. Place the filled dough rolls seam-side down on the prepared baking sheet.
8. Brush the tops of the rolls with melted butter.
9. Bake the Boxty Rolls in the preheated oven for 25-30 minutes, or until golden brown and cooked through.
10. Remove the rolls from the oven and let them cool slightly before serving.

These Boxty Rolls are delicious served warm with your favorite fillings, such as cooked bacon, sautéed mushrooms, sliced cheese, cooked sausage, or any other fillings you prefer. They make a tasty and satisfying meal or snack, perfect for any occasion!

Bacon and Potato Bake

Ingredients:

- 6 slices bacon, chopped
- 4 cups potatoes, peeled and thinly sliced
- 1 onion, thinly sliced
- 2 cloves garlic, minced
- 1 cup shredded cheese (cheddar, mozzarella, or your favorite cheese)
- 1 cup heavy cream
- Salt and pepper to taste
- Chopped fresh parsley for garnish (optional)

Instructions:

1. Preheat your oven to 375°F (190°C). Grease a baking dish with butter or cooking spray.
2. In a skillet over medium heat, cook the chopped bacon until crispy. Remove the bacon from the skillet and place it on a plate lined with paper towels to drain excess grease. Set aside.
3. In the same skillet with the bacon fat, add the thinly sliced onions and minced garlic. Cook for 3-4 minutes, or until the onions are softened and translucent. Remove from heat and set aside.
4. In a large mixing bowl, combine the thinly sliced potatoes, cooked bacon, cooked onions and garlic, and shredded cheese. Season with salt and pepper to taste. Toss until well combined.
5. Transfer the potato mixture to the prepared baking dish, spreading it out evenly.
6. Pour the heavy cream over the potato mixture, making sure it's evenly distributed.
7. Cover the baking dish with aluminum foil and bake in the preheated oven for 45-50 minutes, or until the potatoes are tender when pierced with a fork.
8. Remove the foil and bake for an additional 10-15 minutes, or until the top is golden brown and bubbly.
9. Remove from the oven and let it cool for a few minutes before serving.
10. Garnish with chopped fresh parsley, if desired, before serving.

This Bacon and Potato Bake is a delicious and comforting dish that's perfect for a cozy dinner or as a side dish for special occasions. Enjoy its creamy texture and savory flavors!

Irish Sausages with Onion Gravy

Ingredients:

For the sausages:

- 8 Irish pork sausages
- 2 tablespoons olive oil

For the onion gravy:

- 2 large onions, thinly sliced
- 2 tablespoons unsalted butter
- 2 tablespoons all-purpose flour
- 2 cups beef broth
- 1 tablespoon Worcestershire sauce
- Salt and pepper to taste
- Chopped fresh parsley for garnish (optional)

Instructions:

1. Heat the olive oil in a large skillet over medium heat. Add the sausages and cook them for 10-12 minutes, turning occasionally, until they are browned on all sides and cooked through. Once cooked, transfer the sausages to a plate and set aside.
2. In the same skillet, melt the butter over medium heat. Add the thinly sliced onions and cook them for 8-10 minutes, stirring occasionally, until they are soft and caramelized.
3. Sprinkle the flour over the caramelized onions and stir to combine. Cook for 1-2 minutes, stirring constantly.
4. Gradually pour in the beef broth, stirring constantly to prevent lumps from forming. Add the Worcestershire sauce and season with salt and pepper to taste.
5. Bring the gravy to a simmer and cook for 5-7 minutes, or until it has thickened to your desired consistency.

6. Return the cooked sausages to the skillet with the onion gravy. Reduce the heat to low and let them simmer in the gravy for 5-7 minutes to heat through and absorb the flavors.
7. Once heated through, remove the sausages from the skillet and transfer them to a serving platter.
8. Spoon the onion gravy over the sausages, garnish with chopped fresh parsley if desired, and serve hot.

This Irish sausages with onion gravy dish is delicious served with mashed potatoes and steamed vegetables on the side. It's a comforting and satisfying meal that's sure to be a hit with family and friends!

Beef and Stout Stew

Ingredients:

- 2 lbs (about 900g) beef chuck or stewing beef, cut into 1-inch cubes
- Salt and pepper to taste
- 2 tablespoons all-purpose flour
- 2 tablespoons olive oil
- 2 onions, chopped
- 4 cloves garlic, minced
- 2 carrots, peeled and sliced
- 2 celery stalks, sliced
- 2 tablespoons tomato paste
- 2 cups stout beer (such as Guinness)
- 4 cups beef broth
- 2 bay leaves
- 1 teaspoon dried thyme
- 1 teaspoon dried rosemary
- 2 tablespoons Worcestershire sauce
- 2 tablespoons cornstarch (optional, for thickening)
- Chopped fresh parsley for garnish (optional)

Instructions:

1. Season the beef cubes with salt and pepper. Place them in a large bowl and sprinkle with flour, tossing to coat evenly.
2. In a large Dutch oven or heavy-bottomed pot, heat the olive oil over medium-high heat. Add the beef cubes in batches and brown them on all sides. Remove the browned beef cubes and set them aside.
3. In the same pot, add the chopped onions, minced garlic, carrots, and celery. Cook for 5-6 minutes, stirring occasionally, until the vegetables are softened.
4. Stir in the tomato paste and cook for another 1-2 minutes.
5. Return the browned beef cubes to the pot. Pour in the stout beer and beef broth, stirring to deglaze the pot and scrape up any browned bits from the bottom.
6. Add the bay leaves, dried thyme, dried rosemary, and Worcestershire sauce to the pot. Stir to combine.

7. Bring the stew to a boil, then reduce the heat to low. Cover the pot and let the stew simmer gently for 2-3 hours, or until the beef is tender and the flavors have melded together.
8. If you prefer a thicker stew, you can mix 2 tablespoons of cornstarch with 2 tablespoons of cold water to make a slurry. Stir the slurry into the stew and let it simmer for an additional 10-15 minutes, or until thickened.
9. Taste the stew and adjust the seasoning with salt and pepper if necessary.
10. Serve the Beef and Stout Stew hot, garnished with chopped fresh parsley if desired.

This Beef and Stout Stew is rich, flavorful, and deeply satisfying. Serve it with crusty bread, mashed potatoes, or over rice for a complete meal. Enjoy its hearty goodness!

Kerry Apple Cake

Ingredients:

- 2 cups all-purpose flour
- 1 teaspoon baking powder
- 1/2 teaspoon baking soda
- 1/2 teaspoon ground cinnamon
- 1/4 teaspoon ground nutmeg
- 1/4 teaspoon salt
- 1/2 cup unsalted butter, softened
- 3/4 cup granulated sugar
- 2 large eggs
- 1 teaspoon vanilla extract
- 1/2 cup buttermilk
- 2 cups apples, peeled, cored, and chopped (such as Granny Smith or Golden Delicious)
- Confectioners' sugar for dusting (optional)

Instructions:

1. Preheat your oven to 350°F (175°C). Grease and flour a 9-inch (23cm) round cake pan or line it with parchment paper.
2. In a medium bowl, whisk together the all-purpose flour, baking powder, baking soda, ground cinnamon, ground nutmeg, and salt. Set aside.
3. In a large mixing bowl, cream together the softened butter and granulated sugar until light and fluffy.
4. Beat in the eggs, one at a time, until well combined. Stir in the vanilla extract.
5. Gradually add the dry ingredients to the wet ingredients, alternating with the buttermilk, beginning and ending with the dry ingredients. Mix until just combined.
6. Gently fold in the chopped apples until evenly distributed throughout the batter.
7. Pour the batter into the prepared cake pan and spread it out evenly with a spatula.
8. Bake the Kerry Apple Cake in the preheated oven for 35-40 minutes, or until a toothpick inserted into the center comes out clean and the top is golden brown.

9. Remove the cake from the oven and let it cool in the pan for 10 minutes. Then, transfer it to a wire rack to cool completely.
10. Once cooled, dust the Kerry Apple Cake with confectioners' sugar, if desired.
11. Slice and serve the Kerry Apple Cake on its own or with a dollop of whipped cream or a scoop of vanilla ice cream for an extra treat.

This Kerry Apple Cake is perfect for dessert or as a sweet treat with a cup of tea or coffee. Enjoy its moist and flavorful texture, filled with chunks of delicious apple!

Irish Brown Bread

Ingredients:

- 2 cups whole wheat flour
- 1 cup all-purpose flour
- 1 teaspoon baking soda
- 1 teaspoon salt
- 1 1/2 cups buttermilk
- 2 tablespoons honey or brown sugar
- 2 tablespoons unsalted butter, melted (optional, for brushing)

Instructions:

1. Preheat your oven to 425°F (220°C). Grease and flour a 9-inch (23cm) round cake pan or line it with parchment paper.
2. In a large mixing bowl, whisk together the whole wheat flour, all-purpose flour, baking soda, and salt.
3. In a separate bowl, mix together the buttermilk and honey or brown sugar until well combined.
4. Make a well in the center of the dry ingredients and pour the buttermilk mixture into the well.
5. Stir the ingredients together with a wooden spoon until a rough dough forms. Do not overmix.
6. Turn the dough out onto a lightly floured surface and knead it gently until it comes together, about 1-2 minutes.
7. Shape the dough into a round loaf and place it in the prepared cake pan.
8. Use a sharp knife to score a cross on top of the loaf, about 1/2-inch deep.
9. Bake the Irish Brown Bread in the preheated oven for 15 minutes. Then reduce the oven temperature to 400°F (200°C) and continue to bake for another 25-30 minutes, or until the bread is golden brown and sounds hollow when tapped on the bottom.
10. Remove the bread from the oven and transfer it to a wire rack to cool.
11. If desired, brush the top of the bread with melted butter while it's still warm.
12. Let the Irish Brown Bread cool completely before slicing and serving.

This Irish Brown Bread is delicious served with butter and jam, alongside soups and stews, or as a hearty accompaniment to any meal. Enjoy its rustic flavor and dense texture!

Smoked Salmon with Brown Bread

Ingredients:

- Thinly sliced smoked salmon
- Irish brown bread (homemade or store-bought)
- Cream cheese or crème fraîche
- Lemon wedges
- Fresh dill, chopped (optional)
- Capers (optional)
- Red onion slices (optional)

Instructions:

1. If you're using homemade Irish brown bread, slice it into thin slices. If you're using store-bought brown bread, you can use it as is or slice it if desired.
2. Spread a thin layer of cream cheese or crème fraîche on each slice of brown bread.
3. Arrange slices of smoked salmon on top of the cream cheese or crème fraîche.
4. Squeeze a wedge of lemon over the smoked salmon to add a fresh citrus flavor.
5. If desired, sprinkle some chopped fresh dill over the smoked salmon for extra flavor.
6. Garnish the smoked salmon with capers and red onion slices for additional texture and flavor, if desired.
7. Serve the smoked salmon with brown bread immediately as an appetizer or part of a brunch spread.

This smoked salmon with brown bread is elegant, delicious, and easy to prepare. It's perfect for entertaining guests or for a special weekend brunch at home. Enjoy the combination of rich smoked salmon and hearty brown bread!

Boxty Pancakes with Smoked Salmon

Ingredients:

For the Boxty Pancakes:

- 1 cup grated raw potatoes
- 1 cup mashed potatoes
- 1 cup all-purpose flour
- 1 teaspoon baking powder
- Salt and pepper to taste
- 1/2 cup milk
- 2 tablespoons unsalted butter, melted
- 1 egg, lightly beaten
- Butter or oil for frying

For Serving:

- Thinly sliced smoked salmon
- Cream cheese or crème fraîche
- Fresh dill, chopped
- Lemon wedges
- Capers (optional)
- Red onion slices (optional)

Instructions:

1. Start by preparing the Boxty Pancakes. In a large mixing bowl, combine the grated raw potatoes, mashed potatoes, all-purpose flour, baking powder, salt, and pepper.
2. In a separate bowl, whisk together the milk, melted butter, and beaten egg.
3. Gradually pour the wet ingredients into the dry ingredients, stirring until a smooth batter forms. Add more milk if necessary to achieve a pancake batter consistency.
4. Heat a non-stick skillet or griddle over medium heat. Add a small amount of butter or oil to the skillet.

5. Pour about 1/4 cup of the batter onto the skillet for each pancake. Use the back of a spoon to spread the batter into a circle.
6. Cook the pancakes for 2-3 minutes on each side, or until golden brown and cooked through. Transfer the cooked pancakes to a plate and cover them with a clean kitchen towel to keep warm while you cook the remaining pancakes.
7. Once all the pancakes are cooked, assemble them by spreading a layer of cream cheese or crème fraîche on each pancake.
8. Top each pancake with thinly sliced smoked salmon.
9. Garnish the smoked salmon with chopped fresh dill and a squeeze of lemon juice.
10. If desired, add capers and red onion slices on top for extra flavor and texture.
11. Serve the Boxty Pancakes with smoked salmon immediately as a delicious appetizer or part of a brunch spread.

These Boxty Pancakes with smoked salmon are elegant, flavorful, and perfect for any occasion. Enjoy the combination of fluffy pancakes with luxurious smoked salmon and creamy toppings!

Irish Coffee Cake

Ingredients:

For the Cake:

- 1 cup unsalted butter, softened
- 1 1/2 cups granulated sugar
- 2 large eggs
- 2 teaspoons vanilla extract
- 2 cups all-purpose flour
- 1 teaspoon baking powder
- 1/2 teaspoon baking soda
- 1/4 teaspoon salt
- 1 cup strong brewed coffee, cooled
- 1/4 cup Irish whiskey

For the Glaze:

- 1/4 cup strong brewed coffee, cooled
- 2 tablespoons Irish whiskey
- 2 cups confectioners' sugar

Instructions:

1. Preheat your oven to 350°F (175°C). Grease and flour a 9x13-inch (23x33cm) baking pan or line it with parchment paper.
2. In a large mixing bowl, cream together the softened butter and granulated sugar until light and fluffy.
3. Beat in the eggs, one at a time, until well combined. Stir in the vanilla extract.
4. In a separate bowl, whisk together the all-purpose flour, baking powder, baking soda, and salt.
5. Gradually add the dry ingredients to the wet ingredients, alternating with the brewed coffee and Irish whiskey, beginning and ending with the dry ingredients. Mix until just combined.

6. Pour the batter into the prepared baking pan and spread it out evenly with a spatula.
7. Bake the Irish Coffee Cake in the preheated oven for 30-35 minutes, or until a toothpick inserted into the center comes out clean and the top is golden brown.
8. While the cake is baking, make the glaze. In a small bowl, whisk together the brewed coffee, Irish whiskey, and confectioners' sugar until smooth.
9. Once the cake is done baking, remove it from the oven and let it cool in the pan for 10 minutes.
10. While the cake is still warm, poke holes all over the top of the cake using a skewer or fork.
11. Pour the glaze evenly over the warm cake, allowing it to soak into the holes.
12. Let the cake cool completely in the pan before slicing and serving.

This Irish Coffee Cake is moist, flavorful, and perfect for serving as a dessert or a sweet treat with a cup of coffee. Enjoy its rich coffee and whiskey-infused flavor!

Irish Leek and Potato Gratin

Ingredients:

- 2 tablespoons unsalted butter
- 3 leeks, white and light green parts only, thinly sliced
- 3 cloves garlic, minced
- 2 pounds potatoes, peeled and thinly sliced (such as Yukon Gold or Russet)
- 2 cups shredded Irish cheddar cheese (or your favorite cheese)
- 1 1/2 cups heavy cream
- Salt and pepper to taste
- Chopped fresh parsley for garnish (optional)

Instructions:

1. Preheat your oven to 375°F (190°C). Grease a 9x13-inch (23x33cm) baking dish with butter or cooking spray.
2. In a large skillet, melt the butter over medium heat. Add the sliced leeks and minced garlic, and sauté for 5-6 minutes, or until the leeks are softened.
3. Layer half of the thinly sliced potatoes in the bottom of the prepared baking dish, overlapping slightly.
4. Spread half of the sautéed leeks and garlic mixture over the layer of potatoes.
5. Sprinkle half of the shredded cheese over the leeks and potatoes.
6. Repeat the layers with the remaining potatoes, leeks, and cheese.
7. In a small saucepan, heat the heavy cream over medium heat until warm. Season with salt and pepper to taste.
8. Pour the warm cream evenly over the layers of potatoes, leeks, and cheese in the baking dish.
9. Cover the baking dish with aluminum foil and bake in the preheated oven for 45-50 minutes, or until the potatoes are tender when pierced with a fork.
10. Remove the foil and bake for an additional 10-15 minutes, or until the top is golden brown and bubbly.
11. Remove the gratin from the oven and let it cool for a few minutes before serving.
12. Garnish the Irish Leek and Potato Gratin with chopped fresh parsley, if desired, before serving.

This Irish Leek and Potato Gratin is rich, creamy, and packed with flavor. It's perfect as a side dish for St. Patrick's Day or any special occasion. Enjoy its comforting goodness!

Rhubarb Crumble

Ingredients:

For the filling:

- 4 cups chopped rhubarb (about 1-inch pieces)
- 1/2 cup granulated sugar
- 2 tablespoons all-purpose flour
- 1 teaspoon vanilla extract
- Zest and juice of 1 orange (optional)

For the crumble topping:

- 1 cup old-fashioned oats
- 1/2 cup all-purpose flour
- 1/2 cup brown sugar
- 1/2 teaspoon ground cinnamon
- 1/4 teaspoon salt
- 1/2 cup unsalted butter, cold and diced

Instructions:

1. Preheat your oven to 375°F (190°C). Grease a 9x9-inch (23x23cm) baking dish or any similar-sized baking dish.
2. In a large mixing bowl, combine the chopped rhubarb, granulated sugar, all-purpose flour, vanilla extract, and orange zest and juice (if using). Toss until the rhubarb is evenly coated in the sugar mixture.
3. Transfer the rhubarb mixture to the prepared baking dish and spread it out evenly.
4. In another mixing bowl, combine the old-fashioned oats, all-purpose flour, brown sugar, ground cinnamon, and salt. Mix well.
5. Add the cold diced butter to the oat mixture. Using your fingertips or a pastry cutter, rub the butter into the dry ingredients until the mixture resembles coarse crumbs and the butter is evenly distributed.
6. Sprinkle the crumble topping evenly over the rhubarb filling in the baking dish.

7. Place the baking dish in the preheated oven and bake for 35-40 minutes, or until the rhubarb is bubbling and the crumble topping is golden brown and crispy.
8. Remove the rhubarb crumble from the oven and let it cool for a few minutes before serving.
9. Serve the rhubarb crumble warm, topped with a scoop of vanilla ice cream or a dollop of whipped cream if desired.

This rhubarb crumble is a delightful dessert that's perfect for showcasing the tangy flavor of rhubarb. Enjoy its sweet and crunchy goodness!

Boxty Fritters

Ingredients:

- 2 cups grated raw potatoes
- 1 cup mashed potatoes
- 1 cup all-purpose flour
- 1 teaspoon baking powder
- 1/2 teaspoon salt
- 1/4 teaspoon black pepper
- 1/4 cup chopped fresh parsley (optional)
- 2 eggs, lightly beaten
- 1/4 cup milk
- Vegetable oil for frying

Instructions:

1. In a large mixing bowl, combine the grated raw potatoes, mashed potatoes, all-purpose flour, baking powder, salt, black pepper, and chopped fresh parsley (if using). Mix well to combine.
2. In a separate bowl, whisk together the eggs and milk until well combined.
3. Pour the egg and milk mixture into the potato mixture and stir until a thick batter forms. If the batter seems too thick, you can add a little more milk to reach the desired consistency.
4. Heat vegetable oil in a large skillet or frying pan over medium heat.
5. Once the oil is hot, drop spoonfuls of the potato batter into the hot oil, making sure not to overcrowd the pan. Flatten the fritters slightly with the back of a spoon.
6. Fry the fritters for 3-4 minutes on each side, or until golden brown and crispy. You may need to adjust the heat to prevent them from burning.
7. Once the fritters are cooked through and golden brown, remove them from the oil using a slotted spoon and transfer them to a plate lined with paper towels to drain excess oil.
8. Repeat the process with the remaining batter until all the fritters are cooked.
9. Serve the boxty fritters hot, accompanied by your favorite dipping sauce or condiment, such as sour cream, applesauce, or ketchup.

These boxty fritters are crispy on the outside, soft and fluffy on the inside, and full of delicious potato flavor. They make a fantastic appetizer, side dish, or snack, perfect for any occasion!

Irish Cheese Platter

Ingredients:

Cheese Selection:

- Dubliner Cheese: A semi-hard cheese with a rich, nutty flavor and a slightly sweet undertone.
- Cashel Blue Cheese: A creamy and tangy blue cheese with a delicate flavor and a smooth texture.
- Irish Cheddar Cheese: Opt for a mature Irish cheddar, which has a sharp and robust flavor profile.
- Gubbeen Cheese: A semi-soft cheese with a complex flavor that ranges from nutty to earthy.

Accompaniments:

- Soda Bread or Brown Bread: Serve slices of traditional Irish soda bread or brown bread alongside the cheeses.
- Fresh and Dried Fruits: Include apples, pears, grapes, and figs for a variety of flavors and textures.
- Nuts: Offer a variety of nuts such as almonds, walnuts, and hazelnuts for added crunch.
- Chutney or Jam: Serve a selection of chutneys, jams, or preserves such as fig, pear, or apple to enhance the flavors of the cheeses.
- Honey: Drizzle some honey over the cheeses for a touch of sweetness.
- Crackers or Crispbread: Provide a selection of crackers or crispbread for guests to enjoy with the cheeses.
- Olives: Add some briny olives to the platter for a savory contrast to the cheeses.

Instructions:

1. Arrange the cheeses on a large serving platter or wooden board, leaving space between each cheese.
2. Label each cheese with a small sign or marker to help guests identify them.

3. Place the accompaniments around the cheeses, grouping similar items together.
4. Add some fresh herbs or edible flowers for garnish and color.
5. Serve the Irish cheese platter alongside a selection of Irish beers, ciders, or whiskeys for a complete tasting experience.
6. Encourage guests to explore the flavors and textures of the cheeses, pairing them with different accompaniments to discover their favorite combinations.
7. Enjoy the Irish cheese platter as a delicious appetizer or as part of a cheese tasting experience with friends and family!

This Irish cheese platter recipe allows you to showcase the unique and delicious flavors of Irish cheeses while providing a variety of accompaniments to complement them.

Enjoy the flavors and textures of Ireland's finest cheeses!

Dubliner Cheese and Onion Tart

Ingredients:

For the Tart Crust:

- 1 1/4 cups all-purpose flour
- 1/2 teaspoon salt
- 1/2 cup unsalted butter, cold and cubed
- 3-4 tablespoons ice water

For the Filling:

- 2 tablespoons unsalted butter
- 3 large onions, thinly sliced
- 1 teaspoon granulated sugar
- Salt and pepper to taste
- 1 cup Dubliner cheese, grated
- 3 large eggs
- 1 cup heavy cream
- 1/4 teaspoon ground nutmeg
- Fresh thyme leaves for garnish (optional)

Instructions:

1. Preheat your oven to 375°F (190°C).
2. To make the tart crust, in a food processor, combine the all-purpose flour and salt. Add the cold cubed butter and pulse until the mixture resembles coarse crumbs.
3. Gradually add the ice water, 1 tablespoon at a time, and pulse until the dough comes together and forms a ball.
4. Transfer the dough to a lightly floured surface and shape it into a disk. Wrap it in plastic wrap and refrigerate for at least 30 minutes.

5. Roll out the chilled dough on a lightly floured surface into a circle large enough to fit into a 9-inch tart pan. Press the dough into the pan and trim any excess. Prick the bottom of the crust with a fork.
6. Line the tart crust with parchment paper and fill it with pie weights or dried beans. Blind bake the crust in the preheated oven for 15 minutes. Remove the parchment paper and weights and bake for an additional 5 minutes, or until the crust is golden brown. Remove from the oven and let it cool slightly.
7. While the crust is baking, prepare the filling. In a large skillet, melt the butter over medium heat. Add the thinly sliced onions and cook, stirring occasionally, until they are soft and caramelized, about 20-25 minutes.
8. Sprinkle the caramelized onions with sugar, salt, and pepper, and continue to cook for another 5 minutes.
9. Spread the caramelized onions evenly over the partially baked tart crust. Sprinkle the grated Dubliner cheese over the onions.
10. In a mixing bowl, whisk together the eggs, heavy cream, and ground nutmeg until well combined. Pour the egg mixture over the onions and cheese in the tart crust.
11. Return the tart to the oven and bake for 25-30 minutes, or until the filling is set and the top is golden brown.
12. Remove the tart from the oven and let it cool slightly before serving. Garnish with fresh thyme leaves, if desired.
13. Serve the Dubliner Cheese and Onion Tart warm or at room temperature, sliced into wedges.

This Dubliner Cheese and Onion Tart is perfect for brunch, lunch, or a light dinner. Enjoy its rich and savory flavors!

Potato Bread

Ingredients:

- 1 cup mashed potatoes (about 2 medium potatoes, peeled, boiled, and mashed)
- 1/4 cup unsalted butter, melted
- 1/4 cup granulated sugar
- 2 1/4 teaspoons active dry yeast (1 packet)
- 1/4 cup warm water (110°F/45°C)
- 1 cup warm milk (110°F/45°C)
- 1 teaspoon salt
- 4-5 cups all-purpose flour

Instructions:

1. In a small bowl, dissolve the active dry yeast in warm water. Let it sit for 5-10 minutes, or until foamy.
2. In a large mixing bowl, combine the mashed potatoes, melted butter, sugar, warm milk, and salt.
3. Add the yeast mixture to the potato mixture and stir until well combined.
4. Gradually add the all-purpose flour, one cup at a time, stirring until a soft dough forms.
5. Turn the dough out onto a lightly floured surface and knead for 8-10 minutes, or until the dough is smooth and elastic. Add more flour as needed to prevent sticking, but keep in mind that the dough should still be slightly sticky.
6. Place the dough in a greased bowl, turning once to coat, and cover with a clean kitchen towel or plastic wrap. Let it rise in a warm, draft-free place for 1-1.5 hours, or until doubled in size.
7. Punch down the risen dough and turn it out onto a lightly floured surface. Divide the dough in half and shape each half into a loaf.
8. Place the shaped loaves into greased loaf pans, cover, and let rise again for 30-45 minutes, or until doubled in size.
9. Preheat your oven to 375°F (190°C).
10. Bake the risen loaves in the preheated oven for 25-30 minutes, or until the bread is golden brown and sounds hollow when tapped on the bottom.
11. Remove the loaves from the oven and transfer them to wire racks to cool completely before slicing.

12. Serve the potato bread sliced and enjoy it fresh with butter or as a delicious addition to sandwiches.

This homemade potato bread is soft, moist, and perfect for enjoying as a side with soups, stews, or as part of a hearty breakfast. Enjoy its comforting flavor and texture!

Irish Lamb Shank with Mint Sauce

Ingredients:

For the Lamb Shank:

- 4 lamb shanks
- Salt and pepper to taste
- 2 tablespoons olive oil
- 2 onions, chopped
- 2 carrots, chopped
- 2 celery stalks, chopped
- 4 garlic cloves, minced
- 2 tablespoons tomato paste
- 2 cups beef or lamb stock
- 1 cup red wine (optional)
- 2 sprigs fresh rosemary
- 2 sprigs fresh thyme
- 2 bay leaves

For the Mint Sauce:

- 1/2 cup fresh mint leaves, finely chopped
- 1/4 cup white wine vinegar
- 1 tablespoon granulated sugar
- Salt and pepper to taste

Instructions:

1. Preheat your oven to 325°F (165°C).
2. Season the lamb shanks generously with salt and pepper.
3. Heat the olive oil in a large oven-safe Dutch oven or braising pan over medium-high heat. Add the lamb shanks and brown them on all sides, about 5-6 minutes per side. Remove the lamb shanks from the pan and set them aside.

4. In the same pan, add the chopped onions, carrots, and celery. Cook, stirring occasionally, until the vegetables are softened and lightly browned, about 5-7 minutes.
5. Add the minced garlic and tomato paste to the pan, and cook for another 1-2 minutes, stirring constantly.
6. Return the lamb shanks to the pan and pour in the beef or lamb stock and red wine (if using). Add the fresh rosemary, thyme, and bay leaves to the pan.
7. Cover the pan with a lid and transfer it to the preheated oven. Braise the lamb shanks in the oven for 2.5 to 3 hours, or until the meat is tender and falls off the bone.
8. While the lamb shanks are cooking, prepare the mint sauce. In a small bowl, combine the finely chopped mint leaves, white wine vinegar, sugar, salt, and pepper. Stir until the sugar is dissolved. Set aside to allow the flavors to meld.
9. Once the lamb shanks are done cooking, remove them from the oven and transfer them to a serving platter. Cover loosely with aluminum foil to keep warm.
10. Strain the cooking liquid from the pan through a fine mesh sieve into a saucepan. Skim off any excess fat from the surface of the liquid. Bring the liquid to a simmer over medium heat and cook until it reduces and thickens slightly, about 10-15 minutes.
11. Serve the lamb shanks hot, drizzled with the reduced cooking liquid and accompanied by the mint sauce.
12. Enjoy your Irish Lamb Shank with Mint Sauce with your favorite side dishes, such as mashed potatoes, roasted vegetables, or crusty bread.

This Irish Lamb Shank with Mint Sauce is tender, flavorful, and sure to impress your guests. Enjoy the delicious combination of tender lamb with the refreshing mint sauce!

Boxty with Fried Eggs

Ingredients:

For the Boxty:

- 2 cups grated raw potatoes
- 1 cup mashed potatoes
- 1 cup all-purpose flour
- 1 teaspoon baking powder
- 1/2 teaspoon salt
- 1/4 teaspoon black pepper
- 1/4 cup milk
- 2 tablespoons unsalted butter, melted
- Vegetable oil for frying

For Serving:

- Eggs
- Salt and pepper to taste
- Fresh chopped chives or parsley for garnish (optional)

Instructions:

1. In a large mixing bowl, combine the grated raw potatoes, mashed potatoes, all-purpose flour, baking powder, salt, and black pepper.
2. Add the milk and melted butter to the potato mixture and stir until well combined. The batter should have a thick consistency, similar to pancake batter. If it's too thick, you can add a little more milk.
3. Heat a non-stick skillet or frying pan over medium heat and add a little vegetable oil.
4. Spoon the Boxty batter into the skillet to form pancakes, using about 1/4 cup of batter for each pancake. Use the back of a spoon to spread the batter into circles.

5. Cook the Boxty pancakes for 3-4 minutes on each side, or until golden brown and crispy. You may need to adjust the heat to prevent them from burning.
6. While the Boxty pancakes are cooking, fry the eggs in a separate skillet or frying pan according to your preference (fried, sunny-side up, over-easy, etc.).
7. Once the Boxty pancakes and eggs are cooked, transfer them to serving plates.
8. Season the fried eggs with salt and pepper to taste.
9. Place a fried egg on top of each Boxty pancake.
10. Garnish with fresh chopped chives or parsley, if desired.
11. Serve the Boxty with fried eggs immediately, while still warm.

This Boxty with fried eggs is a satisfying and flavorful dish that's perfect for breakfast, brunch, or even a hearty dinner. Enjoy the combination of crispy potato pancakes with creamy fried eggs!

Roast Chicken with Bacon and Potatoes

Ingredients:

- 1 whole chicken (about 4-5 pounds), giblets removed
- Salt and pepper to taste
- 6 slices bacon
- 1 tablespoon olive oil
- 1 onion, chopped
- 4 cloves garlic, minced
- 1 teaspoon dried thyme
- 1 teaspoon dried rosemary
- 1 teaspoon paprika
- 1/2 teaspoon garlic powder
- 1/2 teaspoon onion powder
- 1/2 teaspoon dried oregano
- 1/2 teaspoon dried parsley
- 4-5 medium potatoes, peeled and quartered
- 1 cup chicken broth or water

Instructions:

1. Preheat your oven to 375°F (190°C).
2. Season the whole chicken inside and out with salt and pepper.
3. Lay the bacon slices on top of the chicken, covering as much of the surface as possible. You can secure the bacon with toothpicks if needed.
4. Heat the olive oil in a large skillet or roasting pan over medium-high heat. Add the chopped onion and minced garlic, and sauté until softened and fragrant, about 3-4 minutes.
5. Add the dried thyme, dried rosemary, paprika, garlic powder, onion powder, dried oregano, and dried parsley to the skillet. Stir to combine and cook for another 1-2 minutes.
6. Place the quartered potatoes in the skillet and toss to coat them in the onion and herb mixture.
7. Push the potatoes to the sides of the skillet to make room for the chicken. Place the bacon-wrapped chicken in the center of the skillet, breast-side up.
8. Pour the chicken broth or water into the skillet, around the chicken and potatoes.

9. Transfer the skillet to the preheated oven and roast the chicken for 1 hour to 1 hour 15 minutes, or until the internal temperature of the chicken reaches 165°F (74°C) and the bacon is crispy.
10. Remove the skillet from the oven and let the chicken rest for 10-15 minutes before carving.
11. Serve the roast chicken with bacon and potatoes, along with the pan juices drizzled over the top.
12. Enjoy your delicious and comforting roast chicken with bacon and potatoes!

This dish is perfect for a cozy family dinner or a special occasion meal. The combination of tender roast chicken, crispy bacon, and flavorful potatoes is sure to be a hit!

Dublin Lawyer Pasta

Ingredients:

- 1 pound (450g) linguine or fettuccine pasta
- 2 lobster tails, thawed if frozen
- 4 tablespoons unsalted butter
- 4 cloves garlic, minced
- 1/4 cup Irish whiskey (such as Jameson)
- 1 cup heavy cream
- Salt and pepper to taste
- Fresh parsley, chopped, for garnish
- Grated Parmesan cheese, for serving (optional)

Instructions:

1. Bring a large pot of salted water to a boil. Cook the pasta according to the package instructions until al dente. Drain the pasta, reserving 1/2 cup of the pasta cooking water.
2. While the pasta is cooking, prepare the lobster tails. Using kitchen shears, cut along the top of each lobster tail shell to expose the meat. Carefully remove the meat from the shells and chop it into bite-sized pieces.
3. In a large skillet or sauté pan, melt the butter over medium heat. Add the minced garlic and cook for 1-2 minutes, until fragrant.
4. Add the chopped lobster meat to the skillet and sauté for 2-3 minutes, until the lobster is opaque and cooked through.
5. Pour the Irish whiskey into the skillet and let it simmer for 1-2 minutes to cook off the alcohol.
6. Stir in the heavy cream and bring the sauce to a simmer. Let it cook for 3-4 minutes, stirring occasionally, until the sauce thickens slightly.
7. Season the sauce with salt and pepper to taste.
8. Add the cooked pasta to the skillet with the lobster sauce. Toss everything together until the pasta is evenly coated with the sauce. If the sauce is too thick, you can add some of the reserved pasta cooking water to loosen it up.
9. Remove the skillet from the heat and garnish the Dublin Lawyer Pasta with chopped fresh parsley.
10. Serve the pasta immediately, with grated Parmesan cheese on the side if desired.

11. Enjoy your delicious Dublin Lawyer Pasta!

This pasta dish is rich, creamy, and packed with flavor, making it perfect for a special dinner or entertaining guests. Serve it with a side salad and some crusty bread for a complete meal.

Chocolate Guinness Cake

Ingredients:

For the Cake:

- 1 cup Guinness stout
- 1 cup unsalted butter, diced
- 3/4 cup unsweetened cocoa powder
- 2 cups granulated sugar
- 3/4 cup sour cream
- 2 large eggs
- 1 tablespoon vanilla extract
- 2 cups all-purpose flour
- 2 1/2 teaspoons baking soda

For the Cream Cheese Frosting:

- 8 oz (225g) cream cheese, softened
- 1/2 cup unsalted butter, softened
- 2 cups powdered sugar, sifted
- 1 teaspoon vanilla extract

Instructions:

1. Preheat your oven to 350°F (175°C). Grease and flour a 9-inch round cake pan or line it with parchment paper.
2. In a saucepan, heat the Guinness stout and diced butter over medium heat until the butter is melted. Remove from heat and whisk in the cocoa powder and granulated sugar until smooth.
3. In a separate mixing bowl, whisk together the sour cream, eggs, and vanilla extract until well combined.
4. Gradually pour the Guinness mixture into the sour cream mixture, whisking constantly until smooth.
5. Sift the flour and baking soda into the wet ingredients and gently fold until just combined. Be careful not to overmix.
6. Pour the batter into the prepared cake pan and smooth the top with a spatula.
7. Bake in the preheated oven for 45-50 minutes, or until a toothpick inserted into the center of the cake comes out clean.

8. Remove the cake from the oven and let it cool in the pan for 10 minutes before transferring it to a wire rack to cool completely.
9. While the cake is cooling, prepare the cream cheese frosting. In a mixing bowl, beat the softened cream cheese and butter until smooth and creamy.
10. Gradually add the powdered sugar, one cup at a time, beating well after each addition. Stir in the vanilla extract.
11. Once the cake has cooled completely, spread the cream cheese frosting over the top of the cake.
12. Slice and serve the Chocolate Guinness Cake, and enjoy!

This Chocolate Guinness Cake is rich, moist, and full of flavor, making it the perfect dessert for St. Patrick's Day or any special occasion. Enjoy it with a cold glass of milk or a cup of coffee for a delightful treat!

www.ingramcontent.com/pod-product-compliance
Lightning Source LLC
LaVergne TN
LVHW061944070526
838199LV00060B/3971